OUR Love LANGUAGE

STORY by **TARA PERRON**
ILLUSTRATIONS by **SIMONE ALEXA**

On the West side of a big city there lived a boy named Tino. Every summer morning he was woken up by a huge slobbery lick from his dog Lablo. Tino wasn't fond of a wet cheek, but he understood this was his dog's love language. Tino was his dog's best friend, and Lablo followed him everywhere he could.

Summers on the West Side were filled with bicycle races with neighborhood kids, penny candy from the corner store, street markets with fresh food, and being home before the streetlights came on.

On Saturday mornings Tino would check his piggy bank and count all the pennies he had saved up for the week. After counting he would yell, "Come on Lablo," then hop on his bike, and ride to the corner store.

Mr. G the store's owner would be outside watering the marigolds or sweeping the walkway. Taking care of the neighborhood was how Mr. G showed his love for the community.

As Tino would park his bike Mr. G would say, "Hola perro." Lablo would give Mr. G a big lick in exchange for a doggie biscuit.

"Mr. G you'll never guess how many pennies I counted today!" Tino would say. Mr. G replied, "I don't know, maybe tres?" Then Tino would say, "Nope, I helped mama rinse the vegetables from the market. She gave me five pennies, and you know what that means!"

Mr. G would go behind the counter and count out five candies from a jar and hand them to Tino. Before Mr. G could even say goodbye Tino was already on his bike and down the street.

He passed by his sisters playing jump rope. He even waved hello to his uncle and dad fixing a car. Tino was the youngest in the family. All of his siblings spent their Saturdays hanging out with friends, but not Tino! He spent his time with Abuela.

As he swung open the screen door at his grandparent's home the aroma of tortillas surrounded him like a big hug. His favorite smell! Abuela turned around from cooking, and with flour all over her hands she pinched Tino's cheeks. "Nieto, te he estado esperando," she told her grandson. Tino loved being at his grandmother's house, because she was always happy to see him.

"Agarrar la silla," she exclaimed and pointed to the corner of the room.

Tino didn't understand Spanish, and had no clue what she was pointing at. So he quickly grabbed the broom.

"No, no," Abuela said with a little laugh. Tino laughed too! Then she gently pulled a stool over next to her. There were many times Tino got mixed up with his grandmother's language, but she was always kind and understanding with him.

Abuela always had something delicious cooking on the stove. Some days it was rice, some days frijoles, and on the weekends it was pozole. Tino loved visiting his Abuela!

There was always family around too. Cousins would stop over to eat, drop off food, or even dance in the living room. Tino admired the family photos that took up every inch of the walls. Some pictures looked 100 years old.

Tino's grandpa always had mariachi music playing, if he wasn't watching his TV shows from his big comfy chair. Some days Tino would play with toy cars on the carpet next to his Abuelo's chair. All grandpa's shows were in Spanish, but Tino still enjoyed listening while he played.

Tino's favorite time at his grandparents house was in the kitchen. Abuela's kitchen was filled with fresh peppers, clay pots, and bright colors everywhere.

"Hagamos tortillas," she would say. Tino nodded because he knew the word tortilla!

"Mezclar la masa," she would tell Tino. Abuela could see the confusion on Tino's face. She would gently put his hands into the dough mixture. Together they would mix the dough. Her hands, his hands, their hands as one.

Everything Abuela made for their family was a form of love, and that needed no translation.

Once the tortillas were finished Abuela would break the tortilla in half. She would give Tino a little, then take a little for herself. Lablo would bark from the front porch because he wanted a little too.

"¿Te gustan las tortillas?" Abuela would ask as she rubbed her tummy. Tino took his last bite and rubbed his tummy too.

His grandmother would always wrap up a stack of tortillas to send home for the rest of the family. Before heading home his grandmother pointed to a dish on the table and said, "Centavos." Tino looked in the dish, then grinned from ear to ear. "Pennies!" he said. Then, he hugged his Abuela goodbye.

Leaving his grandparent's house he felt like the richest boy on the west side!

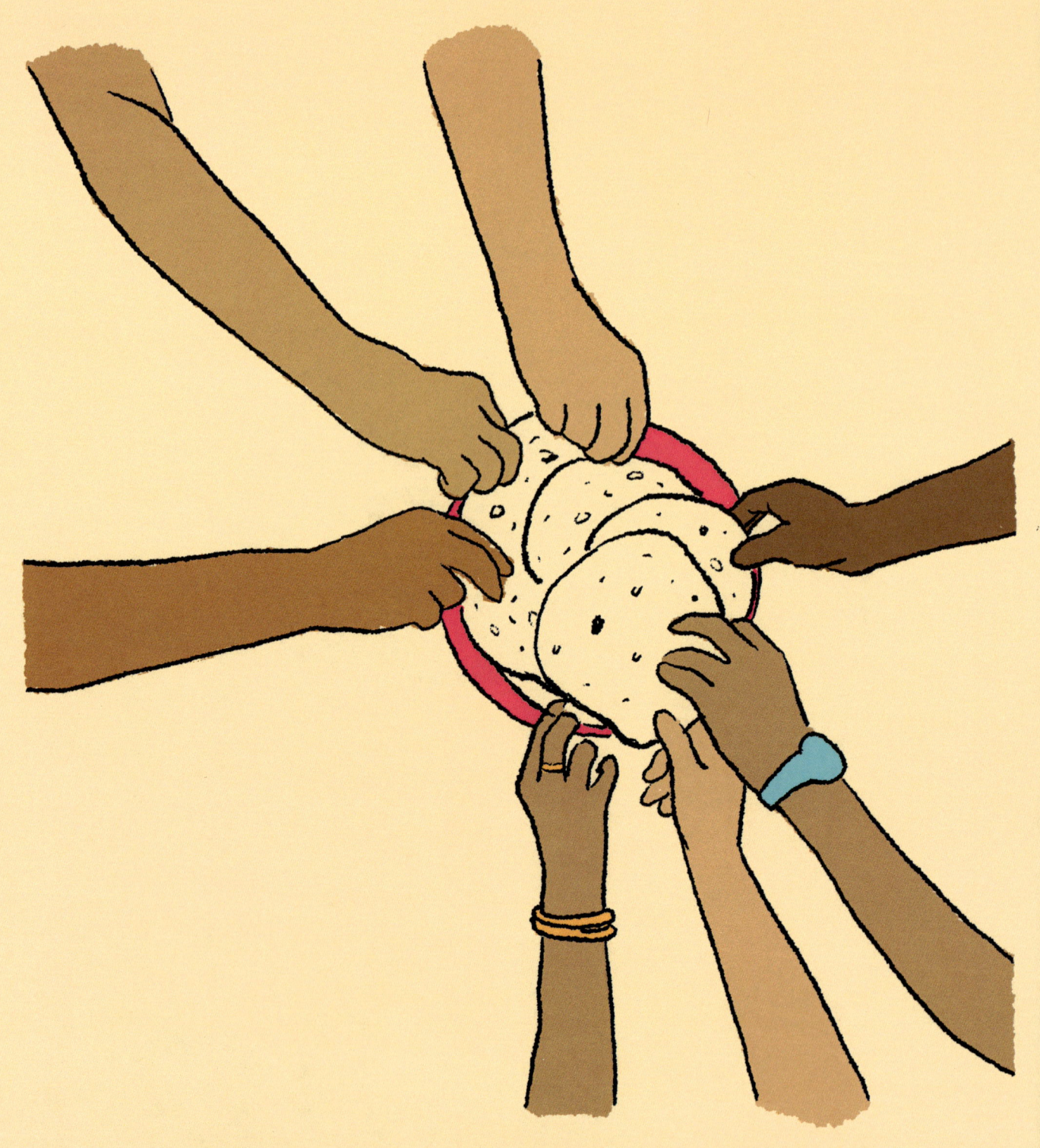

When Tino arrived home he was excited to share the tortillas with his family. Abuela secretly knew her tortillas would bring the family together! Love was the language Tino shared with his abuela! Their relationship was spoken through hugs, laughter, and homemade tortillas. That was a language Tino's heart understood.

Garcia Tortilla Recipe

2½ cups of sifted flour
1 teaspoon of salt
1 teaspoon of baking powder
½ cup of shortening
1 cup of hot water

DEDICATION

Guadalupe and Jesus, you are
forever in our hearts.

Our Love Language

Text copyright ©2023 by Tara Perron
Illustrations copyright ©2023 by Simone Alexa

All rights reserved. No part of this book may be reproduced in any form whatsoever, by photography or xerography or by any other means, by broadcast or transmission, by translation into any kind of language, nor by recording electronically or otherwise, without permission in writing from the author, except by a reviewer, who may quote brief passages in critical articles or reviews.

ISBN: 979-8-9855073-3-1

Tanagidan To Win
BlueHummingbirdWoman.com

Illustrated by Simone Alexa
Book cover and interior design by Paul Nylander | Illustrada